M000027581

The
BEST·MAN
FOR
The Job
IS A
Woman

A BOOK OF **GIRL POWER**

THE BEST MAN FOR THE JOB IS A WOMAN

An exclusive edition for

for all your gift books and gift stationery

This edition first published in Great Britain in 2018 by Allsorted Ltd, Watford, Herts, UK WD19 4BG

All rights reserved. No part of this work may be reproduced in any form or by any means, electronic or mechanical, including photocopying, recording or by any information storage and retrieval system, without the prior written permission of the publisher.

© Susanna Geoghegan Gift Publishing

Author: Roffy
Cover design: Milestone Creative
Contents design: Double Fish Design Ltd

ISBN: 978-1-911517-39-9

Printed in China

THE BEST MAN
For the Job is
★ A WOMAN ★

Let's face it, men have been a bit tricky ever
since the year dot.

Every time Adam came in from a 'night out with the boys',
Eve always thought it best to count his ribs, just in case.

Things are improving though, and the world is slowly
becoming more equal. But do we want complete equality if
that means women can't always be best at everything?

Okay, okay, it would be wrong to constantly make fools of
men - most are the do-it-yourself type anyway.

Rather than put them down, let's instead focus on some
successful women in all walks of life. Over the coming pages,
you'll find the stories behind winning women, the scientific
proof why women rule, and the reality of being a woman in
the modern world. All rounded off with words of wit and
wisdom from inspirational women.

And a few jokes about men, because, well, you know.

So, to sum it all up, the best man to read this book
is a woman.

WOMAN OF MIRTH

5-bark

★ REVIEW ★

Sally owned a small hotel. One day she received an email from someone who wanted to stay there for a weekend. It read:

'I would very much like to bring my dog with me. He is well-groomed and very well-behaved. Would you be willing to permit me to keep him in my room with me at night?'

Sally wrote back, 'I've been operating this hotel for many years. In all that time, I've never had a dog steal towels, bedclothes, silverware or pictures off the walls. I've never had to evict a dog in the middle of the night for being drunk and disorderly. And I've never had a dog run out on a hotel bill. Yes, indeed, your dog is welcome at my hotel. And, if your dog will vouch for you, you're welcome to stay here too.'

· VALENTINA TERESHKOVA ·

Best known as: The first woman in space on June 16, 1963, orbiting the earth 48 times solo in Vostok 6.

Top trivia: Her mission was cloaked in secrecy - her family thought she was taking part in a skydiving competition until they heard her name on the radio.

The rebel: Valentina had eaten very little while in space. Upon landing, against all the official rules, she gave her provisions to nearby villagers and enjoyed their local food in return.

Quotable: *'Hey sky, take off your hat, I'm on my way!'*

Science
OF THE
SEXES

• WOMEN RULE AT MULTITASKING •

In 2010, psychologists at the University of Herefordshire gave 50 male and 50 female students eight minutes to solve maths problems, find restaurants on a map, and devise a plan for locating a lost key in a field - all at the same time.

Each received a phone call during the test with extra general knowledge questions. Women proved more capable of managing all four tasks at once, while men often failed on a strategy to find the key.

Let's face it, if his key is not in his pocket, it's lost for good anyway!

....

· WOMEN RULE AT DRIVING ·

A 2015 study assessed 50 drivers in their cars and observed another 200 at Hyde Park Corner in London. Taking into account 14 different aspects of driving, women scored 23.6 points out of 30, while men only scored 19.8.

One result showed that women were much more likely to use their indicators correctly.

Thinking about it, when are men good at telling us what's on their minds?

....

· WOMEN RULE AT EMPATHY ·

A 2014 study of 20,000 people by Griffith University, Australia, found that when partners were ill or experienced the death of a friend, women were noticeably affected, yet men were not significantly affected by unfortunate events in their partner's life.

So next time you're ill in bed, it's a scientific fact that he'll be more upset that there's no dinner on the table.

WOMAN OF MIRTH

The art of

★ SEDUCTION ★

Mel and her friends are enjoying a bottle of wine
outside a quiet rural pub.

One of them appears at the bar and gestures alluringly to the
barman who comes over immediately. When he arrives, she
signals seductively that he should bring his face close to hers.
When he does so, she begins to gently caress his beard which
is full and bushy. 'Are you the manager?' she asks, softly
stroking his face with both hands.

'Actually, no,' he replies.

'Can you get him for me? I need to speak to him,' she says,
running her hands up beyond his beard and into his hair.

'I'm afraid I can't,' breathes
the barman. 'Is there anything I can do?'

'Yes, there is. I need you to give him
a message,' she continues huskily,
putting a finger on his lips.
'Tell him,' she says, 'there is no
toilet paper in the ladies.'

'I DON'T MIND LIVING IN A MAN'S WORLD AS LONG AS I CAN BE A WOMAN IN IT.'

· MARILYN MONROE ·

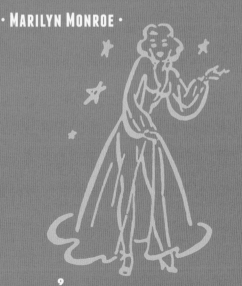

GODDESS vs REALITY

In the

★ KITCHEN ★

Why are there so many cooking shows and celebrity cookbooks? We all know how to cook. Sometimes we just choose not to...

• STARCHY •

Kitchen goddess: To keep potatoes from sprouting in the cupboard, place an apple in the bag with the potatoes.

Kitchen reality: Buy dried mash and keep it until well past the sell-by date.

· SALTY ·

Kitchen goddess: If you accidentally over-salt a dish while it's still cooking, drop in a potato slice.

Kitchen reality: If you accidentally over-salt a dish while it's still cooking, repeat the following: 'I made it and you will eat it'.

· FROTHY ·

Kitchen goddess: Make your own frothy milk for coffee by placing a little milk in a jar, shaking until it's doubled in size, then popping off the lid and microwaving for about 30 seconds.

Kitchen reality: You are never more than five minutes from a Starbucks.

· TIDY ·

Kitchen goddess: When wooden spoons don't look, or smell, like they used to, boil them in a pot of water and leave them in the sun to dry.

Kitchen reality: Buy a new one, or stir with a knife. Carefully.

· BOOZY ·

Kitchen goddess: Freeze leftover wine into ice cubes for future use in casseroles and sauces.

Kitchen reality: Leftover wine? Excuse me?

WOMAN OF MIRTH
Give it a
★ RUB ★

Sally was walking along the beach when she stumbled upon an old fashioned oil lamp. She picked it up and rubbed it, and, surprise surprise, a genie appeared! Sally immediately asked if she was going to receive the standard three wishes.

The Genie said, 'Sorry, but no. Due to inflation, fierce global competition and the unstable economy, I can only grant you one wish. What is your desire?'

Sally didn't hesitate. She said, 'I want peace in the Middle East. See this map? I want these countries to stop fighting with each other.'

The Genie looked at the map and exclaimed, 'Are you kidding me?! These countries have been at war for thousands of years. I'm good, but that's impossible! Make another wish.'

Sally considered possible wishes for a moment, then said, 'I've never been able to find the right man. One who's considerate and fun, enjoys cooking and does their share of the cleaning, is good in bed and gets along with my family, doesn't watch football all the time, and is faithful. Yes, that's what I wish for, that man.'

The Genie let out a long sigh and said, 'Let me have another look at that map...'

Winning Woman

• DOROTHY ARZNER •

Best known as: The only major female director during the 'Golden Age' of Hollywood and the first female member of the Directors Guild of America.

Top trivia: She initially worked as a stenographer for Cecil B. DeMille's brother and worked her way up to become a film editor - in fact she was the first editor to ever be named in a film's credits.

The rebel: Dorothy worked hard to help female actors transition into the new world of 'talkies'. She invented what became known as the boom microphone to help Clara Bow get over her fear of talking on camera.

Quotable: *'When I went to work in a studio, I took my pride and made a nice little ball of it and threw it right out the window.'*

'I DON'T CARE WHO
YOU ARE. WHEN
YOU SIT DOWN TO
WRITE THE FIRST
PAGE OF YOUR
SCREENPLAY, IN
YOUR HEAD, YOU'RE
ALSO WRITING YOUR
OSCAR ACCEPTANCE
SPEECH.'

· NORA EPHRON ·

Exercise
★ CAUTION ★

When they open a new gym next to a patisserie or
a bar, which door do they really expect you to go
through? Don't waste your money on membership.
On a good day, you are already:

Getting the ball rolling

Pushing your luck

Wading through paperwork

Bending over backwards

Balancing the books

Pulling out all the stops

Hitting the nail on the head

Climbing the ladder
of success

EVEN ON A BAD DAY, YOU MIGHT STILL FIND YOURSELF:

Throwing your weight around

Beating around the bush

Jumping to conclusions

Passing the buck

Making mountains out of molehills

Climbing the walls

Running around in circles

Picking up the pieces

You certainly have great flexibility if you can put your foot in your mouth as well!

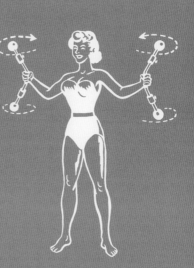

'IF I HAD BEEN AROUND
WHEN RUBENS WAS
PAINTING, I WOULD
HAVE BEEN REVERED
AS A FABULOUS MODEL.
KATE MOSS?
WELL, SHE WOULD
HAVE BEEN THE
PAINTBRUSH.'

· DAWN FRENCH ·

WOMAN OF MIRTH
Missing in
★ ACTION ★

Katie and her husband Will had been out shopping for most of the afternoon.

Suddenly, Katie realised that Will had done that usual man thing and wandered off again. She called his mobile and, somewhat peeved, demanded, 'Where the hell are you?'

Will answered, 'Darling, you remember that jewellery shop where you saw the diamond necklace and totally fell in love with it, and I didn't have money that time so I said, "Hon, it'll be yours one day"?'

Katie smiled, blushed, and said, 'Yes, I remember that, my love.'

Will continued, 'Well, I'm in the bar next door to that shop.'

'THERE'S LOTS OF DIFFERENT **FEMINIST GROUPS.** IT'S NOT AS STRAIGHTFORWARD AS JUST LOOKING **LIKE A PLUMBER.'**

· Jo Brand ·

• INDRA NOOYI •

Best known as: Rising to CEO of PepsiCo in the US after her parents advised her to stay in India, marry and start a family.

Top trivia: When she worked as a dorm receptionist, she took the graveyard shift just so that she could earn an extra 50 cents an hour.

The rebel: Before she left India, Indra played lead guitar in an all-female rock band.

Quotable: *'We need to be treated as equals. I hate to be called "honey" and "sweetie" and "babe". That has to change.'*

21

GODDESS vs REALITY

★ GARDENING ★

Aah, the garden - where you can create a riot of colour and proudly grow your own food, all while getting a bit of exercise in your own little slice of heaven. Or archaeologists keep knocking on your door as they hope to find lost Incan tribes in the overgrown corner of hell you've ignored since you moved in.

· AGRICULTURE ·

Gardening goddess: Grow a wide range of produce throughout the year so you have a fresh supply straight to your table.

Gardening reality: News flash - frozen vegetables exist.

· HORTICULTURE ·

Gardening goddess: Keep a small area of your garden wild to encourage wild flowers, frogs and birds.

Gardening reality: By 'small area' you mean 'all of it'.

· AVICULTURE ·

Gardening goddess: Keeping a few chickens gives you a ready source of eggs, fertiliser and fun!

Gardening reality: Why did the chicken cross the road? To get the hell out of my garden.

· VERMICULTURE ·

Gardening goddess: Place all of your grass cuttings, leaves and garden waste in a compost bin or wormery to create your own natural compost.

Gardening reality: Pile it all behind the shed until it rots through your fence and seeps into your neighbours' kid's sandpit.

· FIZZY-CULTURE ·

Gardening goddess: Just basic garden maintenance means you're outdoors, keeping active and getting a good dose of Vitamin D.

Gardening reality: Cover the garden with artificial grass, then there's a perennial spot for your deckchair and tall glass of gin. Does Vitamin D mix with gin?

WOMAN OF MIRTH

★ CHAOS ★

Kevin returned home from work and found his three children outside, still in their pyjamas, playing in the mud, with empty food boxes and wrappers strewn all around the front garden.

The front door was open and there was no sign of the dog.

In the front room the TV was loudly blaring a cartoon channel, and the floor was strewn with toys and clothes.

In the kitchen, dishes filled the sink, cereal covered the table, the fridge door was open wide and dog food was spilled on the floor.

Kevin went up the stairs, stepping over more toys and clothes, looking for his wife Mandy. He was worried she might be ill, or that something serious had happened.

As he entered the bedroom, he found Mandy curled up in
the bed in her pyjamas, reading a novel.

She looked up at him, smiled, and asked how his day
went. Kevin looked at her bewildered and asked:
'What's going on?'

Mandy continued smiling and answered,
'You know every day when you come home from work
and you ask me what in the world I do all day?'

'Yes?' replied Kevin.

'Well, today I didn't do it.'

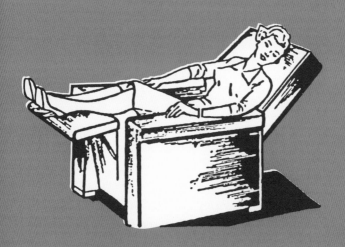

Winning Woman

• CHING SHIH •

Best known as: The most successful pirate of all time, commanding 1,800 ships and 80,000 men.

Top trivia: She married pirate captain Zheng Yi on the condition she took joint control of his fleet. He died a few years later and Ching Shih took over the operation completely, building a fleet that no nation's navy could take down.

The rebel: The Chinese government failed to capture Ching Shih, so in 1810 offered her a pardon if she'd give up her pirate lifestyle. She accepted the offer - then set up a successful casino while bootlegging opium.

Quotable: *'Once a pirate has married a woman, no infidelity against her is permitted. The punishment is beheading.'*

'A WOMAN IS LIKE
A TEA BAG –
YOU NEVER KNOW
HOW STRONG SHE
IS UNTIL SHE GETS
IN HOT WATER.'

· ELEANOR ROOSEVELT ·

QUICK 10

Reasons it's great to be

★ **A WOMAN** ★

Some of these may be obvious, but it's nice to have a reminder.

We never have to reach down every so often to make sure our privates are still there.

We can talk to people of the opposite sex without having pictured them naked.

Women don't think reading the manual is a betrayal of all their gender stands for.

We can congratulate our team-mate without ever touching her butt.

We can see someone cook on a barbecue without feeling the urge to intervene.

The remote control is not an extension of ourselves.

If we get lost, we can ask for directions.

Women know the truth about whether size matters...

We can talk about men in their presence, because they aren't listening anyway!

We can sport a ponytail without looking like an idiot.

'WHATEVER YOU DO,
BE DIFFERENT –
THAT WAS THE ADVICE
MY MOTHER GAVE ME,
AND I CAN'T THINK OF
BETTER ADVICE FOR
AN ENTREPRENEUR.
IF YOU'RE DIFFERENT,
YOU WILL STAND OUT.'

· ANITA RODDICK ·

WOMAN OF MIRTH

No RESERVATIONS

★ ★

A group of 20-year-old girlfriends discussed where they should meet for dinner. They agreed to meet at the Ocean View restaurant because the waiter there had tight trousers and a nice bum.

20 years later at 40 years of age, the group once again discussed where they should meet for dinner. They agreed to meet at the Ocean View restaurant because the food there was very good and the wine selection was excellent.

20 years later at 60 years of age, the group once again discussed where they should meet for dinner. They agreed to meet at the Ocean View restaurant because they could eat there in peace and quiet and the restaurant had a beautiful view of the ocean.

20 years later, at 80 years of age, the group once again discussed where they should meet for dinner. They agreed to meet at the Ocean View restaurant because they had never been there before.

• MARIE CURIE •

Best known as: The first woman to win a Nobel Prize in 1903 and the first ever person to win a second in 1911.

Top trivia: Her research, which led to the discovery of radium and polonium, took place in 'a cross between a stable and a potato shed'.

The rebel: She refused to file patents or profit from her discoveries, instead sharing her work with fellow researchers. By 1920, radium was on sale for $100,000 per gram.

Quotable: *'Be less curious about people and more curious about ideas.'*

'WHATEVER WOMEN DO THEY MUST DO TWICE AS WELL AS MEN TO BE THOUGHT HALF AS GOOD. LUCKILY, THIS IS NOT DIFFICULT.'

· CHARLOTTE WHITTON ·

Science
OF THE
SEXES

· WOMEN RULE AT CLEANLINESS ·

A study by San Diego State University of offices nationwide showed that men's desks contain far more germs than women's desks.

Just in case you've recently had your lunch, we won't go into any more details.

· WOMEN RULE AT BUSINESS ·

A survey of more than 600 board directors by McMaster University, Canada, showed that women are more likely to consider the rights of others and take a cooperative approach to decision-making. Studies by Leeds University in the UK and Catalyst show that boards with high female representation experience 53% higher returns and having just one female director on the board cuts the risk of bankruptcy by 20%.

What? Shouting and bullying is not the route to success?

· WOMEN RULE AT FINANCE ·

A study published by Barclays Wealth shows that female investors tend to achieve a higher return on their investments than men, mainly because testosterone leads to unnecessary risks. A 2005 study by Merrill Lynch said that women also sell off their bad investments quicker than men do.

When was the last time you paid full price for shoes?

WOMAN OF MIRTH

★ CHASER ★

It was a few cocktails into the evening and Kerry was chasing an olive around her glass with a toothpick.

After stabbing at it for the twentieth time she said, 'I give up!'

Her friend Rosie leant over and stuck her toothpick straight into the olive, and, with a cheeky smile, popped it into her mouth.

Kerry scowled and said, 'It was easy for you, I'd tired it out.'

Winning Woman

• TANNI GREY-THOMPSON •

Best known as: Winning 11 gold medals over four Paralympic Games and winning the London Marathon a record six times.

Top trivia: Her real name is Carys, but her two-year-old sister called her 'Tiny' when she first saw her, pronouncing it 'Tanni'. The name stuck, and, even though she is now a Dame, she still uses it today.

The rebel: Tanni has used a wheelchair since she was a young girl due to spina bifida. As a teenager, she was refused admission to a cinema because she was 'a fire risk'. Why, she shot back, did they think she was going to spontaneously combust?

Quotable: *'I get told I'll be able to walk if I eat red kidney beans stewed with pineapple. Then there are those who think I can walk if I really, really try... I try not to bite people's heads off, though.'*

GODDESS vs REALITY

★ THE GYM ★

So you've joined a gym online, but now you realise you actually have to visit it once in a while for it to make a difference.

· GETTING STARTED ·

Gym goddess: Jump out of bed at 5am and jog to the gym as an enjoyable warm up.

Gym reality: You miss 90% of your classes because you're hungover.

· GETTING DRESSED ·

Gym goddess: Look great in your new lycra outfit that makes you feel a million dollars on the treadmill.

Gym reality: You only have one pair of leggings that you always forget to wash between sessions.

· GETTING FRIENDLY ·

Gym goddess: You'll make a new group of workout friends to exercise and chat with.

Gym reality: Realise the only other gym member you can keep up with is the naked pensioner who always traps you in the changing rooms.

· GETTING FIT ·

Gym goddess: It's fun to learn about all the state-of-the art equipment and then use it with confidence.

Gym reality: Miss the orientation session (hungover again) and lurk in the corner trying to watch the person before you, without looking too stalkery.

· GETTING NOURISHED ·

Gym goddess: Feel good after your workout with a kale smoothie. Because your body is a temple.

Gym reality: Eat a box of doughnuts. You've earned the credits.

WOMAN OF MIRTH

★ HOLE-IN-ONE ★

Fiona and Jackie were sat in the clubhouse, enjoying a drink after their round of golf.

'I just got a set of clubs for my husband,' said Fiona.

'Good swap,' said Jackie.

'GRAVITY IS THE STORY OF HOW GEORGE CLOONEY WOULD RATHER FLOAT AWAY INTO SPACE AND DIE THAN SPEND ONE MORE MINUTE WITH A WOMAN HIS OWN AGE.'

· TINA FEY ·

Summer
★ BARBECUE ★

It's the time of year when a man decides he can cook. Surely that's a good thing...?

·····································

1. The woman buys the food.

2. The woman makes a salad, prepares vegetables, and makes dessert.

3. The woman prepares the meat for cooking, places it on a tray along with the necessary cooking utensils and sauces, and takes it to the man who is lounging beside the grill - beer in hand.

4. THE MAN PLACES THE MEAT ON THE GRILL.

5. The woman goes inside to organise the plates and cutlery.

6. The woman comes out to tell the man that the meat is burning. He thanks her and asks if she will bring another beer while he deals with the situation.

7. THE MAN TAKES THE MEAT OFF THE GRILL AND HANDS IT TO THE WOMAN.

8. The woman prepares the plates, salad, bread, utensils, napkins, sauces and brings them to the table.

9. After eating, the woman clears the table and does the dishes.

10. Everyone PRAISES THE MAN and THANKS HIM for his cooking efforts.

11. The man asks the woman how she enjoyed her night off and, upon seeing her annoyed reaction, concludes that there's just no pleasing her.

WOMAN OF MIRTH
Still
★ AT IT ★

92-year-old Enid bursts into the recreation room
at the retirement home. She holds her clenched fist
in the air and bellows,

'Anyone who can guess what's in my hand can
have naughty fun with me tonight!'

An elderly gentleman near the window jokes,
'An elephant?'

Enid thinks for a moment and says, 'Close enough.'

Winning Woman

• SISTER ROSETTA THARPE •

Best known as: Fusing gospel and blues to perform rock 'n' roll-style music in the 1940s, well before anyone used the phrase rock 'n' roll.

Top trivia: Her legendary singing and guitar playing influenced many later musicians, including Bob Dylan and Elvis Presley. She played guitar 'windmill' style, 20 years before Pete Townshend of 'The Who' became known for it.

The rebel: In her later years, Sister Rosetta suffered badly with diabetes, losing a leg to the disease. However, she still continued performing in a chair and would often stand and hop to the beat.

Quotable: *'All this new stuff they call rock 'n' roll, why, I've been playing that for years now.'*

In their own
★ WORDS ★

Some men, not many, but some men know the score. We've given this small space over to the few of their kind that make some sense. Occasionally.

···

As usual, there is a great woman behind every idiot.
John Lennon

What would men be without women?
Scarce, sir...mighty scarce.
Mark Twain

See, the problem is that God gives men a brain and a penis, and only enough blood to run one at a time.
Robin Williams

I'm not sexist – I'm not! That's why I let my female workers work longer than the men so they can make the same money.
Al Murray, The Pub Landlord

Women who seek to be equal with men lack ambition.
Timothy Leary

'FEMINISM IS NOT
A FAD. IT'S NOT
LIKE ANGRY BIRDS.
ALTHOUGH IT DOES
INVOLVE A LOT OF
ANGRY BIRDS.
BAD EXAMPLE.'

· BRIDGET CHRISTIE ·

'I DON'T KNOW WHO **ST VALENTINE** WAS, BUT I HOPE HE DIED ALONE, SURROUNDED BY COUPLES.'

· MIRANDA HART ·

QUICK 10
Online
★ DATING ★

After you have swiped right, it's time to start
reading between the lines.

I love travelling and want to go again: I took a gap year and
haven't got a job yet.

I'm new to this: I previously looked down on people
who met online.

Looking for some good banter: I think insults are a suitable
substitute for conversation.

My family is really important to me: I live with my parents.

I don't really know what to write: I've just realised I'm not
very interesting.

I don't watch television: I watch Netflix.

I'm really funny: I repeat jokes that other people say.

I've changed my hair since my photo: It's not me in my photo.

My favourite author is Kazuo Ishiguro: I've never read any
Kazuo Ishiguro.

Looking for my soulmate: Wannabe stalker.

See me after ★ CLASS ★

The saying goes that 'schooldays are the best days of your life'. Whoever came up with that saying clearly never met my Geography teacher. Or ever experienced a cross country run. With my Geography teacher. If you didn't come top of the class, no need to worry as these famous folks' school reports did not show their potential either.

· CHARLOTTE BRONTË, NOVELIST ·

She 'writes indifferently' and 'knows nothing of grammar'.

· DAME JUDI DENCH, ACTOR ·

'Judi would be a very good pupil if she lived in this world.'

· SUE LAWLEY, PRESENTER ·

'I do believe Susan has glue in her plimsolls.'

· HELEN FIELDING, NOVELIST ·

'Helen must learn not to use such flowery language.'

· JILLY COOPER, NOVELIST ·

'Jilly has set herself an extremely low standard which she has failed to maintain.'

· DAME JOAN COLLINS, ACTOR ·

'She seems to lack the confidence to project... it will be "the films" for her and that would be such a pity!'

· JOANNA LUMLEY, ACTOR ·

'She must learn to speak politely when her requests are refused.'

· BERYL BAINBRIDGE, NOVELIST & PLAYWRIGHT ·

'Her knowledge of the subject is so poor as to make one wonder if she is simple minded.'

· DIANA, PRINCESS OF WALES ·

'A defeatist attitude where her weaknesses are concerned... she must try to be less emotional in her dealings with others.'

· SARAH FERGUSON ·

'She must learn that liveliness should cease at lights out.'

WOMAN OF MIRTH

An offer she could

★ NOT REFUSE ★

Helen was sitting at a bar enjoying a drink with her friends when a tall, dark and handsome man entered.

Helen could not take her eyes off him. He noticed her looking at him and walked over.

Before Helen could apologise for staring, he leant over and whispered, 'I'll do anything, absolutely anything that you want me to do for £20. But only on one condition.'

Helen was shocked at such a forward offer, but fascinated, asked what the condition was.

He replied, 'You have to tell me what you want me to do in just three words.'

Helen considered the proposition for a moment, then took a £20 note from her purse, which she pressed into the man's hand.

She looked deeply into his eyes, and slowly and meaningfully said, 'Clean my house.'

'NO NICE MEN ARE GOOD AT GETTING TAXIS.'

· KATHERINE WHITMORE ·

Winning Woman

• JACQUOTTE DELAHAYE •

Jacquotte Delahaye became a pirate in the
17th Century after both her parents died so she could
afford to look after her sick brother.

Top trivia: She led a gang of over a hundred pirates
and together they took over a small Caribbean island
in 1656. She died in a shootout while defending it some
years later.

The rebel: She faked her own death
to avoid the authorities. When she
returned to piracy, she became known
as 'Back from the Dead Red'.

Quotable: *'I couldn't love a man
who commands me, anymore than
I could love one who lets himself
be commanded by me.'*

54

QUICK 10

Reasons dogs are better

★ **THAN MEN** ★

That old saying needs updating: dogs are a woman's best friend.

Dogs do not have problems expressing affection in public.

Dogs always miss you when you are gone.

Dogs look you in the eye when you talk to them.

Dogs can be forced to take a bath when they need one.

Dogs don't complain when you want to go for a walk.

Dogs understand if some of their friends cannot come inside.

Middle-aged dogs don't feel the need to abandon you for a younger one.

Dogs are nice to your relatives.

Dogs don't criticise your friends.

Dogs don't mind if you do all the driving or if you take a wrong turn.

WOMAN OF MIRTH

★ CONFESSIONAL ★

Lisa was maintaining a candlelit vigil by her husband Steve's bedside as he lay dying.

Steve slowly looked up and said weakly, 'I have something I must confess.'

'Shh,' said Lisa. 'There's really no need.'

'No,' insisted Steve, 'I must confess to you so I can die in peace. I slept with your sister, her best friend, your best friend, and your mother!'

'I know,' Lisa replied, 'now just lie there quietly and let the poison take hold.'

'THE PROBLEM WITH PEOPLE WHO HAVE NO VICES IS THAT GENERALLY YOU CAN BE PRETTY SURE THEY'RE GOING TO HAVE SOME PRETTY ANNOYING VIRTUES.'

· ELIZABETH TAYLOR ·

GODDESS vs REALITY

★ CHRISTMAS ★

These days Christmas seems to start in September, and the leftovers last until the following September. Suggest to your true love that from the first day to the twelfth day of Christmas, the only gift you need is a daily gin and tonic.

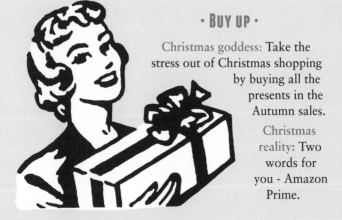

· BUY UP ·

Christmas goddess: Take the stress out of Christmas shopping by buying all the presents in the Autumn sales.

Christmas reality: Two words for you - Amazon Prime.

· SEND UP ·

Christmas goddess: Keep a close eye on the last posting dates before Christmas and beat them by at least a week, just in case.

Christmas reality: Tweet a picture of a turkey in a Christmas jumper on 24th December and say you gave the money saved on cards to charity.

· WRAP UP ·

Christmas goddess: Always use coordinated wrapping paper and ribbon that perfectly match the colour theme of this year's tree decorations.

Christmas reality: Discover the only wrapping paper left in the house says 'Happy Birthday' on it. Use a marker pen to change it to 'Happy Birthday Jesus'.

· MIX UP ·

Christmas goddess: If your Christmas cake recipe needs you to flour the baking tin, use a bit of the dry cake mix instead and there won't be any white mess on the outside of the cake.

Christmas reality: Supermarkets sell Christmas cakes.

· COOK UP ·

Christmas goddess: When you cook the turkey, place a trivet of vegetables and onions in the bottom of the tray to help make the ideal gravy with all the juices.

Christmas reality: Turkey? Gravy? You'd be surprised at how many takeaway shops are open on Christmas Day.

'I LOVE
THE MALE BODY.
IT'S BETTER
DESIGNED THAN
THE MALE MIND.'

· ANDREA NEWMAN ·

• ADA LOVELACE •

Best known as: The world's first computer programmer, writing her first program in 1842-3 for Charles Babbage's Analytical Engine.

Top trivia: The machine was never built so Ada could never test her handwritten program. However, scientists showed in later simulations that her program would have worked perfectly.

The rebel: Her mother encouraged her into mathematics so she would not follow the path of Ada's father, the rebel rousing poet Lord Byron. Ada, however, was keen to unite technology and the arts, calling her work 'poetical science'.

Quotable: *'I am in a charming state of confusion.'*

Science
OF THE
SEXES

· WOMEN RULE AT EDUCATION ·

A study by the University of Georgia in the US found that female students are better at acquiring and retaining knowledge than men. And statistics from the UK and US show that men are more likely than women to drop out of higher education.

Who's going to explain this to the mansplainers?

· WOMEN RULE AT HEALTH ·

A study at McGill University, Canada, in 2009 showed that oestrogen gives women a better natural defence system against bacteria and viruses.

Don't tell men though, otherwise they might want us to take man flu seriously...

· WOMEN RULE AT COMBATTING STRESS ·

Researchers in Ontario, Canada, found that women are far better than men at handling the stress of job interviews. Female brains secrete more oxytocin – otherwise known as the 'cuddle hormone' – than male brains, making women calmer in pressured situations.

Stress: The confusion created when one's mind overrides the body's basic desire to open another bottle of wine.

QUICK 10
Male training
★ SEMINARS ★

If your local college runs any of these evening classes, check if there are any open slots.

Why Sleazy Underthings Are Not Presents

You, Too, Can Do Housework

Mothers-in-Law: They are People Too

You, Too, Can Be a Designated Driver

PMT: Learning When to Keep Your Mouth Shut

Basic Laundry Techniques: formerly titled 'Don't Put my Silks in the Washing Machine'

How Not to Act Like a Jerk When You're Obviously Wrong

How to Go Shopping with Your Mate and Not Get Lost

The Remote Control: Overcoming Your Dependency

'IT IS EASIER TO
DO A JOB RIGHT
THAN TO EXPLAIN
WHY YOU DIDN'T.'

· MARTINA NAVRATILOVA ·

Famous last

★ WORDS ★

No matter what happens during your life,
you get one last chance to say something profound.
These ladies seized the opportunity.

....

It has all been very interesting.
Lady Mary Wortley Montagu

I'm sorry, boys, I'm all wet.
Gracie Allen

Pardon me, sir. I did not do it on purpose.
Marie Antoinette, after stepping on
the foot of her executioner

*I am about to – or I am going to – die:
either expression is correct.*
Dominique Bouhours, French grammarian

Oh, you young people act like old men.
You have no fun.
Josephine Baker

Codeine... bourbon...
Tallulah Bankhead, when asked if she wanted anything

I could shoot better!
Hannie Schaft, to a German soldier
during her execution

Am I dying, or is this my birthday?
Lady Nancy Astor

This sucks.
Agnieszka Osiecka, Polish poet and writer

You see, this is how
you die.
Coco Chanel

Utter nonsense.
Eleanor Roosevelt

If any of you have a
message for the Devil,
give it to me, for I am
about to meet him!
Lavinia Fisher

WOMAN OF MIRTH
Space

★ **INVADER** ★

Once upon a time there was a female brain cell which accidentally ended up in a man's head.

She looked around nervously, but it was all dark, empty and quiet.

'Hello?' she called out.

There was no answer.

She called a little louder, 'Is anyone there?'

Still no answer.

Now the female brain cell started to feel a little scared and yelled at the top of her voice, 'HELLO, IS THERE ANYONE HERE?'

Then she heard a very faint voice from far, far away...

'We're down here...'

'SEIZE THE MOMENT. REMEMBER ALL THOSE WOMEN ON THE TITANIC WHO WAVED OFF THE DESSERT CART.'

· ERMA BOMBECK ·

'WHEN A WOMAN RISES UP IN GLORY, HER ENERGY IS MAGNETIC AND HER SENSE OF POSSIBILITY CONTAGIOUS.'

· MARIANNE WILLIAMSON ·

QUICK 10
Before the
★ BIG TIME ★

Some jobs may not seem very exciting, but who knows what's around the corner? Just see what these 10 women did before their opportunities came knocking.

Whoopi Goldberg had an early job as a bricklayer.

Demi Moore worked as a debt collector.

Jennifer Aniston took to the streets as a bike messenger.

Helen Mirren worked as a promoter for an amusement park.

Rihanna was an army cadet.

Charlize Theron once tended livestock on her parents' farm.

Taylor Swift used to destroy praying mantis pods
in Christmas trees.

Angelina Jolie applied to become a funeral director.

Kim Deal was once a biochemical lab technician.

Four out of the five members of The Long Blondes
were librarians.

WOMAN OF MIRTH
His dad's
★ NOSE ★

Jane and Peter were a middle-aged couple with two beautiful teenage daughters, but they had often talked about having a son.

They decided to try one last time and to their great joy, Jane got pregnant and went on to have a healthy baby boy.

Peter rushed to the baby unit as soon as he could, but was horrified to see his son was the ugliest child he had ever seen. He immediately flew off the handle at Jane, 'There's no way I'm the father of this baby. Look at the two beautiful daughters I fathered! Have you been fooling around behind my back?'

Jane smiled sweetly and replied, 'Not this time...'

Winning Woman

• GABRIELLE 'COCO' CHANEL •

Best known as: Being born in a poorhouse, raised in an orphanage, learning to sew in a convent and then building one of the most successful fashion empires in the world.

Top trivia: In 1921, she released the first perfume to bear the name of a designer. Even though it was her first, she called it Chanel No 5 as she had been told by a fortune teller that this was her lucky number.

The rebel: Money was tight after the First World War, so Coco turned to cheap jersey material to create her distinctive look. Until then, its primary use was for gents' underwear.

Quotable: *'I don't care what you think about me. I don't think about you at all.'*

QUICK 10

Hidden

★ TALENTS ★

A hobby or interest can help keep your mind
off the idiots in your life. These famous names
embrace their inner geek.

Jamie Lee Curtis held
a patent for a nappy
with a built-in waterproof
compartment for
baby wipes.

Leslie Mann can ride
the unicycle.

Ellen Page is a
talented juggler.

Angelina Jolie is a skilled knifethrower.

Susan Sarandon loves ping-pong, opening her own ping-pong nightclub called SPiN in New York City.

Jennifer Garner, in her own words: 'Besides the saxophone, besides playing spoons, besides clogging? Anything hillbilly, I can do.'

Sandra Bullock is fluent in several languages, especially German.

Sarah Michelle Gellar is an expert in tae kwon do.

Christina Hendricks plays the accordion, Halle Berry the flute and Julia Roberts the clarinet.

Geena Davis is a skilled archer, nearly qualifying for the 2000 Olympics.

• LILIAN BLAND •

Best known as: The first person to fly a powered bi-plane in Northern Ireland, in a craft she built by herself after reading about the Wright brothers.

Top trivia: The controls of her plane, 'The Mayfly', were the recycled handles of a bike, and the fuel tank was an empty whiskey bottle, filled with petrol via her deaf aunt Sarah's ear trumpet.

The rebel: Her father feared her aeronautical ambitions, so he promised to buy her a Ford Model T if she would stop flying. Lilian's response? Within a year, she set up Northern Ireland's first Ford dealership.

Quotable: *'A fanatical priest in Tipperary told the people to stone me, but they cheered me on.'*

'ALWAYS CARRY A
BOOK ON A DATE
SO THAT WHEN
YOU GET BORED
YOU CAN SLIP INTO
THE LADIES FOR
A READ.'

• SHARON STONE •

Science

OF THE
SEXES

· WOMEN RULE AT MEMORY ·

A 2015 study at Aston University in the UK discovered that women are better than men at remembering things 2 minutes, 15 minutes, and 24 hours after learning them. Earlier research showed that brain structures important for memory decrease in volume in men, but not in women, between the age of 20 and 40.

Still not a good enough excuse to forget your anniversary though.

· WOMEN RULE AT LIVING ·

Women live about five years longer than men do - in fact 85% of people aged 100 or more are women. Scientists have yet to conclude why, but it may be that tricky testosterone stuff. It might make bodies stronger in the short-term, but it leads to heart disease, infections, and cancer later in life. On the flip-side, oestrogen is an antioxidant, meaning that it can help remove poisonous chemicals inside the body.

Why do men die younger than women? Because women know that good things come to those who wait.

WOMAN OF MIRTH

★ A PRAYER ★

Dear Lord,

So far today I've been on my best behaviour.

I haven't gossiped,

Haven't lost my temper,

Haven't been greedy, grumpy, nasty, selfish, or overindulgent.

But in a few minutes, God,

I'm going to get out of bed.

And from then on,

I'm going to need a lot more help.

Amen

'NEVER REGRET.
IF IT'S GOOD,
IT'S WONDERFUL.
IF IT'S BAD,
IT'S EXPERIENCE.'

· VICTORIA HOLT ·

QUICK 10

Nutritional facts

★ **FANTASY VERSION** ★

We are all trying to be strong, independent women. Then chocolate happens.

If you eat something in front of an open refrigerator or freezer, it doesn't count because you need the extra calories to keep warm.

When you dine with someone else, calories don't count if you eat less than they do.

If you drink a diet cola with a dessert, the calories in the dessert are cancelled out by the diet cola.

Anything you consume at the cinema or a concert contains no calories as it is neither food nor drink.
It is entertainment.

Likewise, anything licked off knives and spoons has no calories if you are in the process of preparing something.
This is not eating: it is cooking.

If you eat something but no one sees you eat it,
it has no calories.

Sausages, cheese and the like are all fattening unless
impaled on frilled toothpicks. The insertion of a sharp
object allows the calories to leak out the bottom.

Food eaten for medicinal purposes does not count.
This includes chicken soup, brandy, hot chocolate and
whole packets of biscuits.

A chocolate mousse that you did not order cannot contain
any calories. Therefore, have your dining companion order
dessert and you taste some/half/all of it.

If you have a drink in your right hand, anything eaten
with the other hand has no calories - this is why it's called
a balanced diet.

'A WOMAN NEEDS ONLY TWO TOOLS IN LIFE: WD 40 AND DUCT TAPE. IF IT DOESN'T MOVE AND IT SHOULD, USE WD 40. IF IT MOVES AND SHOULDN'T, USE THE TAPE.'

· NICOLA ZWEIG ·

Winning Woman

• DELIA DERBYSHIRE •

Best known as: Creating the distinct sound behind the 'Doctor Who' theme tune, and music for over 200 other shows, at the BBC Radiophonic Workshop, introducing a generation to electronic music.

Top trivia: Before the days of digital sampling, Delia would record sounds to tape, speed them up, slow them down and cut them into tiny pieces before sticking them back together to make a final piece of music.

The rebel: She created a soundtrack to camels crossing the Sahara by manipulating a tape of her own voice, overlaid with tapping the side of her favourite lamp.

Quotable: *'What we are doing now is not important for itself, but one day someone might be interested enough to carry things forwards and create something wonderful on these foundations.'*

WOMAN OF MIRTH

When women rule the world

★ THE WORLD ★

When women rule the world,
men will worry about what we are thinking.

When women rule the world,
PMT will be a legitimate defence in court.

When women rule the world,
singles bars will have metal detectors to weed out
men hiding wedding rings in their pockets.

When women rule the world,
during a mid-life crisis, men will get hot flushes
and women will date 19-year-olds.

When women rule the world,
shopping will be considered an aerobic activity.

WOMAN OF MIRTH

When women rule the world,
women with cold hands will give men
prostate examinations.

When women rule the world,
men will not be allowed to eat gas-producing
foods within two hours of bedtime.

When women rule the world,
their 'ideal weight' will be whatever weight they are.

When women rule the world,
men will be judged entirely by their looks,
women by their accomplishments.

When women rule
the world,
all toilet seats will
be nailed down.

• SARAH BERNHARDT •

Best known as: 'The most famous actress in the history of the world', rising to fame on the stages of Europe in the 1870s, having dalliances with Napoleon III and becoming one of the first international film stars.

Top trivia: Imagine Lady Gaga 100 years earlier - Sarah liked to accessorise with a dead bat, never toured without her coffin and once travelled across America accompanied by an alligator called Ali-Gaga.

The rebel: Sarah was convincing in any role - in 1899 she played Hamlet with a skull gifted to her by Victor Hugo. She also starred as the 18-year-old Joan of Arc despite being aged 70 and having a wooden leg.

Quotable: When Oscar Wilde asked her *'Do you mind if I smoke?'*, Sarah replied, *'I don't care if you burn.'*

'THERE MUST
BE QUITE A FEW
THINGS THAT
A HOT BATH
WON'T CURE, BUT
I DON'T KNOW
MANY OF THEM.'

· SYLVIA PLATH ·

The ★ UNANSWERABLE ★

Being a woman is always a full-time job, but if you have any downtime, here are some questions to ponder that men have yet to answer.

Are eyebrows considered facial hair?

If you jog at the speed of sound, can you still hear your iPod?

When does it stop being partly cloudy and start being partly sunny?

If vampires can't see their reflections, why is their hair always so neat?

Why are the smallest possible chocolate bars called 'fun size'?

What do you do when you see an endangered animal that is eating an endangered plant?

If you slap someone with a dictionary, would that be a physical or a verbal assault?

If a Smurf stops breathing, what colour does it turn?

Why do psychics have to ask you your name?

How much deeper would the ocean be without sponges?

If we are what we eat, why aren't we all New,
Improved, and Lite?

What if the Hokey-Cokey really is what it's all about?

Why doesn't Tarzan have a beard?

If a woman's place is in the home, why are
we always in the car?

Does killing time damage eternity?

If one synchronized swimmer drowns, do the
rest have to drown too?

If you ate both pasta and antipasta, would you
still be hungry?

Why don't sheep shrink when it rains?

If Barbie is so popular,
why do you have to buy
friends for her?

Ever notice that the Roman
numerals for 40 are 'XL'?

If ignorance is bliss, why aren't
men always happy?

If Wile E. Coyote had the money
to buy all that ACME stuff, why
didn't he just buy dinner?

What if there were no
hypothetical questions?

WOMAN OF MIRTH

Four-legged

★ FRIEND ★

Jeni was nervous about living alone for the first time so she decided to get a dog for both companionship and protection.

As she looked over a promising hound at the kennels, the breeder told her, 'I must warn you that he doesn't like men.'

'Perfect,' thought Jeni, and she promptly bought the dog.

Some time later as she was walking the dog in the park, two men approached her. Jeni watched to see how her new 'bodyguard' would react. It soon became clear that the breeder hadn't been joking, because as the men got closer, the dog ran under the nearest car and hid.

Winning Woman

• ANITA RODDICK •

Best known as: Founding 'The Body Shop' on the back of her environmental and social ideals.

Top trivia: Even though Anita's company was doing well, she was conflicted over globalisation - in 1999 she was tear-gassed while taking part in the anti-WTO demonstrations in Seattle.

The rebel: The owner of the funeral parlour next door to her first shop complained that her shop's name would hurt their business. Anita responded by leaking a story to the press saying the undertakers were ganging up on a female shopkeeper. Business boomed as readers streamed into her shop to see what all the fuss was about.

Quotable: *'If you think you're too small to have an impact, try going to bed with a mosquito.'*

'THERE IS NO
RECIPROCITY.
MEN LOVE WOMEN,
WOMEN LOVE
CHILDREN, CHILDREN
LOVE HAMSTERS.'

· ALICE THOMAS ELLIS ·

QUICK 10

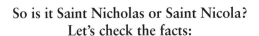

'Father'

★ CHRISTMAS? ★

So is it Saint Nicholas or Saint Nicola?
Let's check the facts:

Santa always remembers Christmas and has never
forgotten to show up, even once.

Santa can pack a bag.

Santa answers their mail.

Santa named the reindeer Cupid and Prancer, not Butch or Arnie.

Santa appreciates home-baked cookies and milk,
not beer and bacon.

Santa doesn't throw presents out of the sleigh to make
room for golf clubs.

Santa keeps detailed lists for each child instead of 'just winging it'.

Santa doesn't wake you up when arriving at midnight,
asking you to make dinner.

And let's face it, a man isn't interested in stockings
unless somebody's wearing them.

WOMAN OF MIRTH

★ VANISHED ★

Bellatrix was a magician who had spent years working on a cruise ship. The audience was different each week so she fell into the habit of performing the same tricks over and over again.

But there was a problem. The captain's parrot saw the shows and slowly noticed how she did them. And once he understood, he started shouting in the middle of the show.

'Squawk! It's not the same hat!'

'Squawk! The flowers are under the table!'

'Squawk! The cards are all the ace of spades!'

Bellatrix was furious, but powerless. It was, after all, the captain's parrot.

Then one stormy night on the Pacific, the ship overturned and sank, drowning nearly everyone on board. Bellatrix found herself on a piece of wood floating in the middle of the sea alongside, as fate would have it, the captain's parrot.

They stared at each other with hatred but did not utter a word.

This went on for a day... two days... then three days.

Finally, on the fourth day, the parrot could not hold back any longer and said, 'Okay, I give up. Where's the bloody ship?'